A Journey Through Grief
Life Beyond the Broken Heart

Julie Yarbrough

Abingdon Press
Nashville

A JOURNEY THROUGH GRIEF:
LIFE BEYOND THE BROKEN HEART
Copyright © 2012 by Julie Yarbrough
All rights reserved.

Scripture passages marked NRSV are taken from the New Revised Standard Version of the Bible, copyright 1989, Division of Christian Education of the National Council of the Churches of Christ in the United States of America. Used by permission. All rights reserved.

Scripture passages marked RSV are taken from the Revised Standard Version of the Bible, copyright 1952 [2nd edition, 1971] by the Division of Christian Education of the National Council of the Churches of Christ in the United States of America. Used by permission. All rights reserved.

Scripture passages marked (NIV) are taken from the Holy Bible, New International Version, NIV®. Copyright © 1973, 1978, 1984, 2011 by Biblica, Inc.™ Used by permission of Zondervan. All rights reserved worldwide. www.zondervan.com. The "NIV" and "New International Version" are trademarks registered in the United States Patent and Trademark Office by Biblica, Inc.™

Scripture passages marked JPB are taken from The New Testament in Modern English © J. B. Phillips 1958, 1960, 1972. MacMillan Publishing Company.

Scripture passages marked AMP are taken from the Amplified® Bible, Copyright © 1954, 1958, 1962, 1964, 1965, 1987 by Lockman Foundation. Used by permission. (www.Lockman.org)

This book is printed on acid-free, elemental chlorine-free paper.

Library of Congress Cataloging-in-Publication Data
Yarbrough, Julie.
 A journey through grief : beyond the broken heart / Julie Yarbrough
 p. cm.
ISBN 978-1-4267-4510-2 (trade pbk. : alk. paper) 1. Consolation. 2 Grief Religious aspects—Christianity. 3. Bereavement—Religious aspects—Christianity. I. Title.
 BV4909.Y37 2012
 248.8'66--dc23   2011041498
   12 13 14 15 16 17 18 19 20 21 — 10 9 8 7 6 5 4 3 2 1
MANUFACTURED IN THE UNITED STATES OF AMERICA

Contents

Introduction

My beloved husband, Leighton Farrell, was Senior Minister at Highland Park United Methodist Church in Dallas, Texas, for twenty-three years. He was the great love of my life. In 2004 he was diagnosed with a terminal disease. Ninety days later he was dead.

Like you, I have faced death in the first person. Though nothing will ever erase the reality of death, grief is not merely enduring what has happened; through our faith it is our personal triumph over tragedy, loss, and death itself. For in grief, pain and sorrow are at last vanquished by our faith; we are healed by God's triumphant adequacy.

On the last occasion that my beloved husband was in the pulpit, he offered this pastoral prayer, which we may claim as a benediction to our grief journey: "We have come this far by faith, and we will continue to walk with our hand in yours wherever you lead us."

On your journey through grief, may the promises of the Bible strengthen and sustain you in the steadfast love and faithfulness of God. In the Holy Spirit there is encouragement and hope for new life beyond the broken heart. Thanks be to God for the victory over death.

1

What Is Grief?

"Very truly I tell you, you will weep and mourn while the world rejoices. You will grieve, but your grief will turn to joy."
John 16:20 NIV

When we experience the pain and heartache caused by the death of our loved one, we delve inside our broken heart and ask, "What is grief?" For many of us, the death of our loved one is like the death of a part of our self. Grief, then, is the outpouring of emotion and pain that expresses how we feel because of what has happened in our life. Grief is our emotional reaction to the event of death.

Perhaps the greater question is "Why do we grieve?" We grieve because we love. We grieve in direct proportion to the depth of our love. The more you love, the greater your grief. The more sensitive you are, the more you suffer. If you did not love, you would not suffer; grief and suffering are inextricably linked.

Suffering leaves an indelible mark on the soul, yet it may be the source of some of the greatest discoveries of life. Through suffering you understand better the things that really matter: the meaning of faith, hope, and love. In suffering you determine whether your faith is a superficial ornament of life or the essential foundation for all of life. In suffering you find your deepest experience of God.

Through faith you are assured that the love you have known with the one who has left this earth will never die. Death has separated you only in body but not in heart. The apostle Paul affirms, "Love knows no limit to its endurance, no end to its trust, no fading of its hope; it can outlast anything. It is, in fact, the one thing that still stands when all else has fallen" (1 Corinthians 13:7-8 JBP). And if you believe that "God is love" (1 John 4:16 NRSV), then you know affirmatively that love is the one thing that still stands when all else has fallen. Take heart. Love can outlast anything.

Whatever your experience of death and loss, likely you would never forego a love that can outlast anything just to avoid the pain of grief. Even in the face of grief you give thanks for having loved so deeply that when death touches your life, you can do nothing for a while except grieve.

There are many common, universal aspects of grief, but above all else, grief is personal. Your experience of grief is like that of no other person. Everyone grieves differently. No amount of resolve or discipline can determine the course of your grief; it is not possible to order grief or will it to be different than it is. The head cannot lead; it must follow the heart.

Grief has a life of its own. It is a restless shadow in the soul, for a while insistent and unavoidable. You soon discern that the dimensions of grief shift from day to day as you contend with the reality of life without your loved one. How you incorporate grief into your life is the challenge of each new day.

Your life is shaped by how you deal with the unalterable circumstance of death. Grief never leaves you where it finds you. It leaves you disillusioned or more profound. It leaves you fearful or more confident in the faithfulness of God, depending on how intently you listen to what grief has to say. In a sermon Leighton affirmed, "What God expects of us is trust, a loyalty that does not demand full understanding, and a love that dares to trust God even when it cannot fully comprehend where our pain and misery and sorrow are leading us."

If you believe that it is not God's intention that you suffer forever, how, then, do you help yourself through the suffering of grief?

First, be intentional about patience. There is perhaps no spiritual discipline more difficult than patience. We live in an age that insists on instant gratification and quick results—now. Patience is a gift of grief, a discipline taught by grief. It is listening—"Be still, and know that I am God" (Psalm 46:10 NRSV). Patience is waiting in faith for God's will to unfold in your life.

Second, surrender your will to God's will in prayer. You will find relief from your suffering when you ask for God's help in prayer—when there are no words except, "Lord, help me" (Matthew 15:25 NRSV). When you acknowledge in prayer that you are not in control of life or death, you experience a humbling moment in grief. Through prayer you grow spiritually; you are transformed and renewed. When you pray,

- God listens.
- God hears you.
- God answers you.
- God reaches into your heart with abiding comfort and strength.
- God knows your feelings.
- God is never threatened by your emotions, especially those of grief.
- God longs for you to be open and honest.
- God wants to comfort you in this darkest hour of your life.
- God is trustworthy.
- God understands your grief.

Many grieving Christians feel guilty for crying or being sad, their rationale being that persons of strong faith should feel happy to know that their loved one is in heaven. But grief is not a crisis of faith; it is a crisis of the heart. You can believe beyond doubt that your loved one is with God, but you are human. You are in pain. You hurt.

This does not mean that your faith is weak. Rather, grieving is really a show of faith. You trust God to hold you at your most vulnerable, when your life is in pieces and your strength is gone. God is with you as you grieve. God shares your tears and sadness. God feels your pain and sorrow. God is with you as you struggle in your brokenness. Rest in the assurance of Deuteronomy 33:27: "The eternal God is your refuge, and underneath are the everlasting arms" (NIV).

"Now is your time of grief, but I will see you
again and you will rejoice, and no one
will take away your joy."
John 16:22 NIV

2

The Journey of Grief

Even though I walk through the valley
of the shadow of death,
I fear no evil; for thou art with me.
Psalm 23:4 RSV

The experience of grief is often referred to as a journey. If you think about it, a journey is usually longer and more difficult than a short trip. Grief is, in fact, a very personal, solitary, journey of the heart and soul.

We are comforted by the psalmist's familiar, beloved words: "Even though I walk through the valley of the shadow of death, I fear no evil, for thou art with me" (Psalm 23:4 RSV). In this scripture, the image is that of the shepherd guiding his sheep through many terrains and perils to reach hillside grazing and safety. The psalmist makes it personal, "Even though I walk through the valley of the shadow of death." He uses the first person, "I."

We know that the one who dies goes through that symbolic valley toward the finality of death, yet we as survivors actually go through the valley of the shadow of death. We encounter this place of powerful metaphor as we descend the depths to meet our wounded soul at its most vulnerable. We scale the crags of loss and adjustment and at last make our way through our personal valley of the shadow of death to the other side of grief.

Yet we do not know the destination of our grief journey. Have you ever set out on a trip without some idea of where you were going, the best way to get there, or when you would arrive? The unknown path of our journey through the valley of the shadow of death is that which makes grief so arduous.

Along the way we have a front-end collision with anger. We meet up with our fears, which accompany us for part of the journey. We navigate the perilous places of worry and suffering. We detour around and through the unexpected setbacks of grief. Or, we take an unplanned side trip through illness or disability.

Our emotional ups and downs keep us on the uneven pavement of a bumpy road. Our interactions with those who do not understand our grief isolate us on the rough shoulders of a narrow, less-traveled highway. The murky road looms ahead with no end in sight. Its large, garish billboards shout, "What is my destination?" "When will I be there?" "How will I know when I am there?"

The question of grief, then, is this: "How do we traverse the valley of the shadow of death?" The psalmist is clear. He shares the wisdom of his experience with us, saying, "Even though I walk." We are not asked to jog, run, or race. We walk. In 2 Corinthians 5:7 we read, "For we walk by faith, not by sight" (RSV).

Our journey through grief, then, is slow, laborious foot work.

- We put one foot in front of the other, often only one half-step at a time. We walk by faith.
- We lose our balance. We miss a step. Our footing slips. We fall down. We get back up in faith.
- We recover our toehold and again inch forward, gaining ground after each setback. We walk in faith.

We may attempt great bounding strides to deal with our grief as quickly and expeditiously as possible, but despite our efforts grief simply will not be hurried or circumvented; there is no easy detour around grief. Rather, the slow, steady pace of a rhythmic walk will ultimately see us through to the other side of grief. Along the way we acquire the courage and strength for life after loss.

You may be new to the emotional time travel of grief, still reliving every footstep of the journey and counting the days and weeks since the death of your loved one like mile markers along the road.

Perhaps you have been on the road for months—maybe even years—weary from the endless road ahead. When you pause from time to time to assess where you are in grief, you look in the rearview mirror of your life for a better view of the past. Although time does not necessarily "heal all," as many well-intentioned comforters like to assure you when you grieve, time does allow you to reflect on both the past and the future. Your hard-won perspective is the compass that points the way toward fullness of life, your promise for the future.

The geography of grief includes places and settings that will never again be the same without your loved one. Along the way, your head and heart signal your direction—where to go, what to avoid. Your head may say "go"; your heart may say "broken–stop–don't go." As the geography of grief changes from deep valley to expansive plain, it may be less painful, perhaps even pleasurable, to revisit places you once abandoned in grief.

As you grieve, you create a personal map that charts where you are going in life without your loved one. Your map may include unknown territory. Unable to imagine life beyond the visible horizon on distant shores—a life in undiscovered places—some early explorers expected to fall off the edge of the earth. Yet the allure of what might lie beyond inspired them to risk everything for an unknown adventure. They embarked on their journeys into the future with faith that God would be there to lead them, light the way, and direct their paths.

God charts the map of your grief journey through the valley of the shadow of death; God faithfully leads you beside still waters and restores your soul. You understand at last that God's divine destination for you at the end of the journey is peace.

In grief, peace does not overwhelm you all at once and for all time. You are not suddenly "there." Peace comes in small, elusive moments as fleeting glints of emotional sunshine that warm and then fade. These moments recur with greater frequency until your life is gradually more about peace than about grief. You will know that you are near the end of the journey when you claim for yourself in gratitude the gift and blessing of God's peace because:

- You have forgiven yourself your human insufficiency to death.
- You no longer strain against that which you cannot change.
- You have traversed the valley of the shadow of death and survived.

The journey through grief is nuanced by contrasts of light and dark, which create shadow. We recognize this in our lives as the long shadow cast by death. "Even though I walk through the valley of the shadow of death . . . " (Psalm 23:4 RSV). Inherent within shadow is the suggestion of light. Without light there can be no shadow. We make our way through the valley of the shadow of death because light is hidden within the shadow. We persevere through grief because at the end of

18

the journey there is the promise of divine radiance and hope.

I walk before the LORD
in the land of the living.
Psalm 116:9 NRSV

3

God's Comfort in Grief

"Blessed are those who mourn,
for they will be comforted."
Matthew 5:4 NRSV

As your grief progresses through the pain of loss and loneliness, the rather counterintuitive promise of the fourth beatitude or "declaration of blessedness" from the Sermon on the Mount assures you that, because you mourn, you will be blessed. Perhaps this is a way to make sense of it: Because you mourn, you are comforted; when you are comforted, then you are, in turn, blessed.

In grief you may struggle to reconcile feeling blessed with mourning. After all, who feels blessed when someone dies? And what is the blessing of death for those of us who remain in this world except the end of mortal pain and suffering for our loved one? Because mourning is the expression of your inmost sorrow, grief insists that you mourn before you are blessed with authentic comfort. Rest assured that because you mourn, you will be comforted.

Comfort means "with strength." To be comforted, then, is to be made strong. In the distress of grief, your comfort and strength are from the Holy Spirit, who never leaves you: "And I will ask the Father, and He will give you another Comforter . . . that He may remain with you forever" (John 14:16 AMP). When we grieve, our hearts are attuned to the power and presence of the Holy Spirit, the One who can "comfort those in any trouble" (2 Corinthians 1:4 NIV). The Holy Spirit strengthens you in affirmation of the promise of eternal life: "I am the resurrection and the life" (John 11:25 NRSV). Through the pain of grief, your source of spiritual comfort is the Holy Spirit, who comforts all who mourn and provides for those who grieve. In comfort you are strengthened; through faith you have life. God comforts you in your grief.

A comforter is one who consoles. Your comforter is anyone who can comfort you in the trouble and pain of your grief. If you are a parent or if, as a child, you had someone in your life who lavished comfort on you, you have had the human experience of unconditional love and spiritual care. This is the mirror of God's love for you as you grieve. God's comfort is not just a promise; it is the absolute assurance of God's understanding, presence, and all-embracing care for you. God knows your grief.

In grief you better learn to understand and forgive your would-be comforters, those who try to console you with empty words or gestures. You expect others to know and understand what you are feeling, but it is not possible. You alone appreciate the depth of your personal experience of grief. The truth is that no one can comfort you to your expectations; nor can you grieve to the expectations of another. Grief is not a job with a performance standard. Comfort is yours to reject or receive. God comforts you as you grieve.

There are many nuances of comfort that sometimes qualify your grief. Perhaps you are experiencing the "dis-comfort" of mental and bodily distress as you struggle to adjust, adapt, and accept the death of your loved one. Or, if you are overwhelmed by grief, you may be truly "un-comfort-able," that is, unable to receive comfort from others or even from God. For a while, it is not possible for you to be comforted by anyone or anything. Your soul may refuse to be comforted because your deepest desire is not comfort as much as it is the return of life as it was.

How, then, do you open your heart to receive comfort? One way is through praising God in prayer. The Psalms include a wealth of prayers poured out in praise of God, such as these verses:

> *Who, O God, is like you?*
> *Though you have made me see troubles,*
> *many and bitter,*
> *you will restore my life again;*
> *from the depths of the earth*
> *you will again bring me up.*
> *You will increase my honor*
> *and comfort me once again.*
> Psalm 71:19-21 NIV

Comfort is not a one-time treatment or cure for grief. In grief, your need is for repeated comfort—again and yet again. With each expression of comfort, likely you experience at least a momentary peace. Comfort relieves your pain; comfort affirms and restores your life. As in

Psalm 71, comfort brings you up again from the depths of grief.

As you explore and develop your instinct for self-comfort, you better understand that which truly comforts you in moments "beside the still waters" (Psalm 23:2 RSV). You actively participate in your own comfort when you consciously transform the discomfort of grief into hope. In comfort and strength, lift up your heart toward new life:

- Be thankful for the gift of life.
- Read for grief understanding and spiritual enrichment.
- Write in a journal to reflect within your inmost heart. Words show where you have been and give direction for the future.
- Find a spiritual or social support community. Share your story with others in a safe environment of care and compassion.
- Find a confidential grief friend who listens with kindness and empathy.
- Relieve isolation and loneliness by reaching out to others.
- Pray for renewal and personal transformation. "Rejoice in hope, be patient in suffering, persevere in prayer" (Romans 12:12 NRSV).

- Stay connected to the world; it is not waiting on you or for you.

In a sermon on "Grief and Death," Leighton said, "Our lives are in the hands of a loving, caring, merciful God. God cares about us. God cares about us in our moments of grief; God cares about us in our moments of death. I can commend to you a God who loves you, cares about you, who will hold you in His arms if you will let Him." As he spoke, he poured the power and passion of his faith into the word *cares*. Neither he nor I could know at that time that his words of grace and comfort were meant for me. God cares about you.

You grieve toward growth when you rest in the grace of God at work in your life, through the power of the Holy Spirit to comfort and strengthen your heart. God uses grief to teach you more of God's comfort through the gift of his steadfast love. You suffer for a while, yet you are assured of God's love as he comforts you. The unimaginable depth and breadth of God's infinite love is your comfort in grief.

Let your steadfast love become my comfort.
Psalm 119:76 NRSV

4

The Grace of Acceptance

We know that in everything God works
for good with those who love him,
who are called according to his purpose.
Romans 8:28 RSV

As you journey through grief, you follow the path through the valley of the shadow of death. First, you descend to its depths; then, slowly but surely, you ascend, always following the upward path toward acceptance. Yet on the way to acceptance, you perhaps pause for a moment to take a final backward glance. You remember the dark sadness, sorrow, and emotional turmoil of compelling grief that once held you captive. As you adjust through grief, you slowly let go of the physical life that once was. But you will never forget, ever. Your earthly life together was real.

Nothing can void what you experienced in your lifetime together with your loved one, however long or short. What lies behind is your history; it is part of who you will yet become.

The past informs the rest of the life you have been given to live. Though it may seem so for a while, you did not die physically when your loved one died. Your purpose and destiny did not die with the one who is gone. In acceptance you cherish the unforgettable, build on the past, and hold on to all that gives value and worth to life, conformed to the reality of the present. On the other side of grief, at last you see clearly where you have been and what you have been through. You complete the journey of grief because you have dared to travel this lonely, deserted road of the heart.

Acceptance is the emotional maturing of your adjustment to life as it is becoming. When adjustment becomes the norm, you move resolutely toward acceptance. You accept that your loved one is physically gone and acknowledge this as permanent. You understand what happened and know that the outcome cannot be changed. Though you do not like it, reluctantly, you accept it. As you have so faithfully done in grief, you work at acceptance. Perhaps you are able to time-date a moment of acceptance, or acceptance may simply occur. You approach acceptance when you at last acknowledge that you are no longer actively grieving.

A prerequisite to acceptance is the realization that you never will be able to fully comprehend some things. God alone understands life and death. Acceptance is, in part, a slow metamorphosis of the mind. The mental ordering of grief occurs simultaneously, though perhaps not precisely in tandem, with the physical, emotional, and spiritual acceptance of death. In fact, your thoughts determine who you are and how you live. Grief encourages a kind of conscious hyper-vigilance of the mind. When you deconstruct your subconscious walls of self-protection and live again in open, free exchange with others and the world, you arrive at acceptance. When the thoughts of your mind find expression in words, you hear what grows inside after the death of your loved one. They speak of that which dwells deep within. Acceptance speaks peace. Acceptance speaks love. Acceptance speaks gratitude for the gifts of grief and the gift of life.

But if you allow grief to defeat your spirit,

acceptance may be a dull resignation that has little to do with hope and faith. As you near acceptance, then, it is well to search the closed-off corners of your mind for the lingering remnants of grief. With the death of your loved one, it is understandable that for a while negative thoughts easily overwhelm the positive. Yet life lived in chronic negativity is life lived in darkness. Acceptance cannot penetrate darkness; it thrives on light.

Acceptance is retraining your mind to accommodate both the absence and abiding presence of your loved one. In acceptance, you transcend physical loss and embrace the spirit of that person's life and love that remains with you always. As adjustment slowly shifts to acceptance, the cold reality of absence is eased by the certainty of enduring love: "Love and faithfulness meet together, righteousness and peace kiss each other. Faithfulness springs forth from the earth, and righteousness looks down from heaven" (Psalm 85:10-11 NIV). The whispered spiritual presence of your loved one surrounds you each day, encouraging you to live on and share your legacy of love with others. The core of acceptance is indwelling—the indwelling of the love of your loved one and the indwelling of the love of God.

In acceptance, you believe with certainty that God works in everything for good with those who love God, who are called according to God's purpose (see Romans 8:28). Yet because you are human, you may question how the death of your loved one can possibly be for good in your life. The case for acceptance lies within the prepositions: *in* everything God works *for* good, *with* those who love God.

- God has not ordained your loss and sorrow. Rather, God meets you at your place of brokenness; God is here in everything.
- God uses grief to teach you more of God's faithfulness and steadfast love. God works for good, using that which has changed your life to promote deeper, more profound faith.
- God works with you because you are called according to God's purpose, that is, because you have faith in God's plan for your life.
- God leads you and works with you to shape a life of meaning and purpose.

Everything new is an outward reflection of your growing acceptance. If you buy sheets, decide on a new car, take a trip, or move your place of residence, you affirm acceptance of life as it is. Within the balance of loss and acceptance, equalized by a more mature faith, you sense that your heart is urging you to live forward.

But this one thing I do: forgetting what lies behind and straining forward to what lies ahead, I press on toward the goal for the prize of the heavenly call of God in Christ Jesus.
Philippians 3:13-14 NRSV

Within acceptance lies the promise that there is yet life, that something does lie ahead. Like a thoroughbred racehorse running full out for the finish line, you press on toward the goal for the prize, straining forward toward new life. There is a goal; there is a prize with notes of joy and possibility. When you relax into the future with faith, you claim the prize of the heavenly call of God in Christ Jesus for life today, tomorrow, and evermore.

Finally, acceptance is victory. Acceptance is the strength and power of an unconquerable soul. As clouds of doubt and fear slowly drift away, you find yourself standing at last, reanimated to life in the full sunlight of God's wonderful grace. And in this moment you are assured from within that there is life beyond grief because there is life beyond death.

> *For you have delivered my soul from death,*
> *my eyes from tears,*
> *my feet from stumbling.*
> Psalm 116:8 NRSV

5

The Hope of Grief

For God alone my soul waits in silence,
for my hope is from him.
Psalm 62:5 NRSV

The steady trajectory of grief is hope. It is, in fact, the very nature of the human heart to hope. Yet hope is more than an emotion. You hope because you are a divinely created human being. No matter how dire the circumstances, you continue to hope because you cannot imagine life beyond the death of your loved one. Even if your loved one is hopelessly ill, you continue to hope because you cannot imagine imminent death or how your life will be beyond the death of the one you love.

Yet grief assails your hope; without hope, it is easy to despair. When you despair, you may drift into cynical acceptance or defeated resignation. Hope leaves no room for despair. In faith there is always hope in God.

Why are you downcast, O my soul,
Why so disturbed within me?
Put your hope in God,
for I will yet praise him
My Savior and my God.
Psalm 42:5-6 NIV

Hopelessness is the dark abyss of grief. Perhaps you have struggled with the unfamiliar emotion of hopelessness on your journey through grief, wondering whether there will ever be more to your life again than just the death of your loved one. You may question whether there is yet life ahead, whether there is even a reason to look forward or to hope. The faith of grief inspires you to look heavenward rather than to the grave, to trust that there is hope and a future through the grace of God.

"For I know the plans I have for you," declares
the Lord, "plans to prosper you and not to harm
you, plans to give you hope and a future."
Jeremiah 29:11 NIV

If you think about it, hope is the teaser of headlines. You read the paper expecting good news, yet often the story belies real hope. Without hope, life is bland and uninspired. Hope is the salt that flavors your life; hope is the seasoning that adds spice to your expectation of life.

Hope does not contradict the reality of death or the toll it takes. When life implodes, you are assaulted on every side. Death happens, but it is not final. Death has robbed you of a loved one's companionship, but it can never rob you of his or her love. In the hope of grief you gratefully acknowledge that the past was real but will never be the present again. You remember and perhaps long for what was, yet in hope you know that life is today. This is the present, the only moment that is now to embrace hope and to live in hope.

Hope is the conviction that the desirable is obtainable and events will turn out for the best. It implies perseverance, the belief that a positive outcome is possible even in the face of evidence to the contrary. Hope is based in reality . . .

- Hope is not naïve optimism.
- Hope is not wishful thinking.
- Hope is not a positive attitude.
- Hope is not a passive wish or dream.

Rather, hope is your fear defeated. The hope of grief is confidence in the divine plan of a loving, caring God—the author of all hope. "Now hope that is seen is not hope. For who hopes for what is seen? But if we hope for what we do not see, we wait for it with patience" (Romans 8:24-25 NRSV). You hope because you have faith.

When you at last feel hopeful again, likely you are down the road on your journey through grief. Still, a few questions may be unresolved for you; but you realize that you are ready to cross the threshold toward the future God has planned for you. You look ahead, eager to move forward out of grief and back into the mainstream of life. You believe that there is a future. You sense that life is becoming more hope filled. At last you discern that for which you should hope. You dare to entertain the idea of joy. You reach out to life in hope—and with hope.

It is among God's mysteries that grief, with all its pain and sorrow, can be the most honest and faithful place you will find hope. For a while the hope of grief may feel like tentative renewal, perhaps like life in suspended animation. Life still may feel rather tepid and lukewarm; this may be a quiet phase—a time of readying, resting, and regrouping after the long grief journey. It is a time to breathe, relax, rest, and live one day at a time in the renewal of your hope.

The most active form of your hope is expressed in prayer. In prayer, you entrust the most fervent hopes of your heart to God because you desire restoration to life. You pray for strength to be in the world because you are changed but curiously fortified by the experience of grief. You pray for hope; you pray in hope.

Hope, then, is sacred evidence of expectancy, patience, trust, and faith. In grief we claim the affirmation of 1 Corinthians 13:13 (JBP): "In this life we have three great lasting qualities—faith, hope and love. But the greatest of them is love." If you think about it, hope stands in the middle—its bookends are faith and love. What God has done through faith, hope, and love illuminates what God will do. Hope does not rely on your own aspirations but on God. You hope for the future because the future belongs to God. In Romans 5:5 the apostle Paul proclaims, "And hope does not disappoint us because God has poured out his love into our hearts through the Holy Spirit" (NRSV). In bold declaration of faith, affirm that hope does not disappoint you, for in God, the best is yet to be. This is your faith; this is your future in God. Hope in God.

*May the God of hope fill you with all joy
and peace as you trust in him, so that you
may overflow with hope by the power
of the Holy Spirit.*
Romans 15:13 NIV

6

Healing From Grief

He heals the brokenhearted,
and binds up their wounds.
Psalm 147:3 NRSV

Healing and wholeness are for those willing to be vulnerable enough to be made strong. You may ask, "Is there healing from grief?" Perhaps you wonder how long it will take you to heal from grief—or even if you will heal. Do you actively entertain the possibility of being healed, or are you satisfied to live with a permanently broken heart? The choice is yours; the answer is clear: There is healing from grief.

He welcomed them and spoke to them about the
kingdom of God, and healed those who
needed healing.
Luke 9:11 NIV

The best analogy for healing in grief is the human body. Physical injury causes a wound of finite, reparable damage that can be treated with the expectation of healing. Death wounds the human soul and spirit; it causes you to grieve. For some, the wound is immeasurable—so deep that healing seems impossible. For others, the wound is less severe. The greater the love for the one you have loved and lost, the larger and deeper your wound.

As with any physical injury, the wound of grief must be taken seriously. Honest, accurate assessment facilitates its treatment, both mentally and spiritually. For many, the wound is caused by slow leave-taking after months or years of chronic illness. For others, death is a tragic, gaping wound in need of immediate, acute care. Most wounds of the body can be healed. All wounds of the soul can be healed.

As with the body, you treat your wound with constructive pain relievers:

- Work
- Church
- Community service/voluntarism
- Hobbies
- Recreation

- Travel
- Children, grandchildren, friends

In your moments of acute woundedness, you may resist healing from grief with uncharacteristic but willful stubbornness. You may think that you are broken beyond healing, that you never will be whole again. If this is your personal assessment, you may try to anesthetize your pain with easy remedies. Likely you have found that this does not work. Quick cures seldom last. God is the one true source of restorative relief from the pain of your grief on the way to healing.

One way that you heal from grief is by releasing your emotions through tears. Science reports that crying releases endorphins, brain chemicals that function as pain relievers and mood elevators. Because tears are cathartic, you usually feel better after you have had a good cry. There may be times when you have cried so much that you feel physically spent—at the end of your resources. This is the moment when healing does its best work.

- Tears are the expression of the deep feelings residing beneath the surface of your fragile exterior that words cannot express. When words fail, tears are the messenger.

- Tears are cleansing. They wash away some of the emotions that trouble you in grief.
- Tears are honest. Denying your tears prevents you from working through pain.
- Tears are healing. Crying releases tension and physical distress.

Relentless, unremitting grief is like an infection; it invades the wound of your soul and resists treatment. When grief permanently overwhelms you, it can destroy your very will to live. If your grief is tenacious, spiritual healing may begin only when you affirm, at last, that you want to be made well. You want your journey through grief to be over.

When you are injured, wound dressings are carefully applied to your physical body to promote healing and protect the point of invasion from germs. Similarly, in grief you may slap a figurative bandage on your wound, not so much to promote healing but to protect yourself from additional hurt and pain. Because you may sense that others do not want to see the gaping hole in your spirit—the imperfect part of your life that is grief—you cover it up using your own self-styled emotional first aid:

- For friends, your bandage may be decorated

with ridiculous yellow happy faces that considerately distract them from your grief.

- For children and grandchildren, your bandage is perhaps a "tough strip," designed to be both protective and impervious.
- For others, you perhaps disguise your woundedness with a clear bandage that conceals your hurt yet does not make your injury truly invisible.
- If you are indifferent to appearance, perhaps you apply a clumsy bandage of gauze and tape that is just "good enough."
- Or perhaps you abandon convention altogether and grieve openly, your gaping emotional wound uncovered and visible for all to see.

Healing is not linear. There is no timeline or prescribed cure date for grief. Rather, healing is the gradual process of becoming whole or sound. Assuming that there is some improvement, you risk the smart of momentary pain when your bandage is ripped from the skin—ouch! Likewise, when inevitable remembrance days tear away the protective covering of your grief wound, you are reminded that you are still vulnerable to pain. When your wound is reopened and exposed by occasions and events, you examine the damage and gratefully discern that you are healing from the inside. You realize that revisiting a painful moment is not a complete re-injury; rather, it is a brief uncovering that requires only the fresh bandage of a new day. And one day you at last take off your protective bandage and find that you are well; you see that you are healed, both inside and out.

Spiritual and emotional healing from grief is perhaps best described as recovery. You convalesce for a while and recuperate from grief. Then you turn a corner and forge ahead into life. If you are finding satisfaction again in life, then you are recovering. Likely you have heard yourself say, whether silently or aloud, "I am better," "I want to live," "Life is good," or some other self-talk that is affirmative and positive. This is a sure indication that you are recovering from grief.

As with the physical body, there is a scar forever in your soul to remind you of your grief. It is at first red and tender, and then slowly it fades until it is almost invisible. It is a medical fact that scar tissue becomes the strongest part of your body. As your spirit slowly heals from grief, you become strongest in your broken places—within the very fiber of your soul. The scar, a spiritual and emotional symbol of your most acute pain, is now part of who you are. Your scar affirms the best part of your own immortality: your soul. The certainty of life after death and life beyond death both assures and comforts your healing heart. Though for a while you are wounded by the death of your loved one, your broken heart one day is healed by the grace of God, the Great Physician. You are living proof of God's power to heal the brokenhearted from grief.

"I will heal my people and will let them enjoy abundant peace and security."
Jeremiah 33:6 NIV

7

How Long Does Grief Last?

*Wait for the L*ORD*;*
be strong, and let your heart take courage;
*wait for the L*ORD*!*
Psalm 27:14 NRSV

The answer to this question is an ongoing discovery as you confront and resolve your own personal issues of grief. Though grief is an inevitable part of life, no one grieves in the same way or at the same pace. Your grief is personal. Grief does not follow the calendar; it cannot be neatly confined to a set number of weeks or months. Although grief is many things, it is not a straight-line experience. Grief comes and it goes; it ebbs and it flows. Imperceptibly, you learn to live alongside grief, but it usually lasts longer than most who grieve expect; grief will not be rushed.

If you think about it, the infrastructure of life consists of both beginnings and endings. Like many, perhaps you, too, want to control the "when" of both the beginning and the ending of most things in life. Because grief is your emotional reaction to the event of death, its onset and end are unique and individual. Each person starts at a different point. For example, grief may have had its beginning as an undertow that swelled through stages of illness, crashing onto the shore of your well-ordered life as the end of life neared. Whatever the circumstance, when and how grief begins may affect how long grief lasts.

Because grief defies an exact moment, your instinct may be to ignore it rather than to enter into it. Some who have experienced the death of a loved one choose simply to hang on mindlessly until grief is over. In fact, you do not enter into grief. Grief enters into you. You move from "Why did this happen?" to "How will I go on?" You experience disbelief and shock and then the reality of life without your loved one.

As the forward dynamic of life gradually redirects your grief, you become more immersed in the positive, life-sustaining memories of your relationship with your loved one than in the unalterable fact of death. For some, it may take several years to work through profound loss and grief. For others, there may be a defining moment such as remarriage that clearly signifies the end of grief. Because your emotions do not conform to life's infrastructure, the end of grief is personal. How long your grief lasts is an intimate process of self-determination. You grieve as long as you grieve.

You may ask, "Is there a 'shelf life' for grief?" For anyone who has experienced death in the first person, the answer is assuredly no. Figuratively, you may box up and shelve your unresolved issues for a while. But some time later, from the improved perspective of time, you probably will decide to take down the box and revisit its content. You may look through what is there and touch it again. Perhaps you will hold it close and reexamine it. You may decide to let it go or hold onto it and put it back on the shelf. Or you may decide to file it, put it in another box of odds and ends, shred it, scrap it, or put it on a figurative bonfire and burn it. This is the only real "shelf life" that pertains to grief. Unlike well-marked packages at a supermarket, grief has no expiration date. Grief lasts as long as it lasts.

Although it is not usually so, in some instances grief may last a lifetime. Queen Victoria made a public and private career of long-term grief as the eternal widow of Windsor. When her husband Albert died, the Queen's grief was profound.

She did not appear in public for three years and wore mourning clothes for over ten years. Her subjects thought her response to death exaggerated, shocking, and abnormal because she would not be moved from her grief. An entire nation expected her to abandon her grief and "get on with life." She suffered from chronic, prolonged depression, and was physically crippled by her grief. She never recovered; she grieved without apology or explanation until she died. Victoria grieved for a lifetime; there was no "shelf life" to her grief.

If you are stuck or meandering on the journey through grief rather than moving forward, your "no end in sight" emotional turmoil may require the insight of another. It may be time for you to seek the help of a confidential, non-judgmental counselor, therapist, or minister who will listen thoughtfully to understand your grief. The guidance of a qualified professional may be critical for understanding the specific, individual issues that may be blocking the resolution of your grief.

Although there are no instructions on how long grief lasts, in John 16:19 (NIV) Jesus tells us that we will grieve for "a little while." Gratefully, "a little while" is not forever. Your assurance is that your grief and pain will not last forever, that you will be restored and made whole again. Though grief may linger in some small dimension as a whisper in your heart, someday you will find yourself unexpectedly wavering between the past and the future and sense that the end of your journey through grief is near.

Though it may not seem so, you have acquired both wisdom and understanding on your journey through grief. Because you have loved and lost, you are entrusted with inestimable gifts that grief gives to you. When you attune your inmost heart to the gifts of grief, you discern with gratitude every manifestation of God's faithfulness to you. As you near the end of the journey through grief, you affirm that God has a purpose for you while you yet have breath on this earth. You learn that you best honor your loved one when you actively reenter the world to endow others with the gifts of your grief as the finest expression of life beyond the broken heart. You honor the steadfast love of God when you resolve to live the rest of the life that is yours empowered by your own extraordinary gifts of grief.

In the certainty of your spiritual growth and enrichment through grief, you thirst again for the adventure of life, ready to rediscover vitality after a long and precarious absence from the world. You have lived through and survived the experience of grief. You rejoin life in the fullness for which God created you. Your night of weeping is at last over.

Weeping may linger for the night,
but joy comes with the morning.
Psalm 30:5 NRSV

8

Choose Life

Now choose life, so that you and your children
*may live and that you may love the L*ORD *your*
God, listen to his voice, and hold fast to him.
*For the L*ORD *is your life.*
Deuteronomy 30:19-20 NIV

Because God endows you with the capacity to
think and reason, choice is part of your everyday
existence and behavior. You choose because you
are alive. If you think about it, you make hundreds
of mindless choices each day: what to wear, what
to do, where to go, whom to see. Many difficult
choices seem imperative after the death of your
loved one, a time when you are most vulnerable.
Choice suggests that there are options, things that
you may decide between or among:

- You may decide not to choose.
  - Why must you choose anything? Mental, emotional, and spiritual inertia occur when grief will not be moved. This choice is for life in an illusory time and space that no longer exists. The assumption of grief is that you are supposed to do something to help yourself in order to survive. If you find yourself stuck, not wanting to be helped in or through your grief, it may be time to seek help.

- You may choose to do nothing.
  - Perhaps your existence is defined only by death. Life lived in memoriam is dedicated solely to the memory of the one who died. This is a meager life with little future—a choice for dying while you are still alive. This is not how your loved one would want you to live.

- You may choose to wait and see.
  - This is a wise choice until, gradually, your life becomes less about pain and sorrow and more about hope for the future. When you are ready, you will experience the urge

to get off the sidelines and reenter life as an active participant. You wait and see, choose and try, and try again until you find a satisfying rhythm of choice.

- You may choose to move forward.
  - The spirit in which you live is a conscious choice. You are in charge of your own emotional destiny. You may choose to live either in chronic misery as the victim of unrelieved sadness turned inward, or in faith, trusting the promise that God has a plan for your future. When you take action, you do something to help yourself: you stretch. When you stretch in grief, you grow toward God. When you embrace anew the rich fullness of life, you are restored to beauty, possibility, and wonder.
  - When you choose to move forward, you plan. You make informed decisions about your own life, but you are not required to make all of tomorrow's choices today.

- You may choose a life of selfless service.
  - "Choose this day whom you will serve . . . but as for me and my household, we will serve the LORD" (Joshua 24:15 NRSV).

54

○ A heart of service thrives in perpetuity. When you serve others in love, you give the gift of yourself.

When the end of your journey through grief nears, it is your responsibility—indeed, your sacred duty of grief—to choose life. You choose, you grow, you live, you love, you serve. "Now choose life. . . . For the LORD is your life" (Deuteronomy 30:19-20 NIV).

When you resolve to choose life, you are then only a small step away from joy. After the long and arduous grief journey, joy is the ultimate quest; it is the final destination of grief. With the death of your loved one, you may feel for a while as though all joy has died. Sadness may become a comfortable habit. The part of you that brimmed with love and joy for the one lost, for life, and for the future seems for a while withered, if not entirely dead. Think of it this way: grief is a season when the branch of your life is dormant. When spring comes again, joy is the ripe, luscious fruit of your carefully tended grief.

As you near the end of grief, you realize perhaps that you have neglected joy along the way. Think about what joy really is, especially from the perspective of your experience of grief.

It looks and feels different now, doesn't it? You may need to devote spiritual energy to relearning joy. In grief this is "re-joicing"— remembering the glory of joy, making joy a habit. Consider joy, practice joy, look for joy. Recall the deep spiritual satisfaction of joy.

Joy beckons you to the other side of grief, calling you to live with renewed enthusiasm and engagement. In that moment of conscious reawakening, love and joy flood your life again with blessing and abandon as you greet the new day of the rest of your life with expectation and hope. Joy is the moment when it is impossible to be silent or wait even one minute longer for new life to burst forth. You want to live again in exuberant joy.

"I have said these things to you so that my joy
may be in you, and that your joy
may be complete."
John 15:11 NRSV

Grief gently teaches you that it is not a betrayal of the one lost to you in death for you to be joyful again in life. Joy may require both practice and discipline of the spirit; joy is a finishing touch to grief. Take up your life where it is. Move beyond grief into life with fullness of joy.

Joy is the balance of peace and hope that resides deep within your human heart and inmost soul. In joy you are at one with God and with yourself, whatever the circumstances of life may be. In joy the noise of insistent grief is at last silent. The light of joy is the beacon of life.

Be glad in the Lord and rejoice, O righteous,
and shout for joy, all you upright in heart.
Psalm 32:11 NRSV

Grief turns to joy when life blossoms in unexpected ways that bring hope for the future. Grief turns to joy with the birth of a child or grandchild. Grief turns to joy in moments that celebrate love. Grief turns to joy with a new partner for the rest of life's journey. And finally, grief turns to joy when at last we are reunited with the one we have grieved in life and in death. From grief comes joy.

Joy, then, is spiritual delight. Joy is the beauty of a roseate sunset. Joy is filtered sunlight through the majesty of trees. Joy is oneness with the moment of life that is this very day. When your belief about death is grounded in faith, you live forward in soul-saturating peace; your soul at last rejoices.

Finally, joy is the enrichment of love. Joy is the uplifting of peace. Joy is the benefit of trust. Joy is the radiance of hope. Joy is the light of faith. Though you can't touch it or feel it or smell it or hold it, joy is the substance of your soul. Reawaken to life in the glory of God's eternal love and joy. Thanks be to God for his faithfulness. As the light of morning dawns, you live again in joy.

You have turned my mourning into dancing;
you have taken off my sackcloth
and clothed me with joy,
so that my soul may praise you
and not be silent.
O Lord my God, I will give thanks
to you forever.
Psalm 30:11-12 NRSV

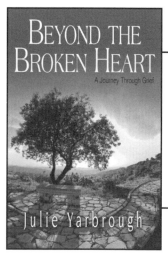

BEYOND THE
BROKEN HEART
A Journey Through Grief

Julie Yarbrough

If you found this booklet helpful and would like more, a small group resource is available from Julie Yarbrough.

Beyond the Broken Heart: A Journey Through Grief is an eight-week support and ministry program for anyone grieving the loss of a loved one. Journeying through each session, participants will experience personal and spiritual growth and enrichment that will transform their grief as their broken hearts are healed by God's gracious love.

Abingdon Press / April 2012

Get more information at:
AbingdonPress.com

About the Author

Julie Yarbrough is a native of Dallas, Texas, and the author of *Inside the Broken Heart.* Inspired by her personal experience after the death of her husband Dr. Leighton Farrell, senior minister at Highland Park United Methodist Church for many years, Julie established a grief support group and began writing articles and books for persons who are grieving.

Julie has published articles in *The United Methodist Reporter, Living with Loss,* and *Grief Digest,* and cooperatively authored the manual *Preparing for Death* for Highland Park United Methodist Church in Dallas, where she is an active member. She also is the author of *Modern Languages for Musicians* and *Peace of Mind: Financial Management for Life,* an estate planning guide. With over thirty years' experience in business management, Julie currently serves as president of Yarbrough Investments.